START YOUR OWN COMPANY

A Step By Step Guide to Start Your Own Company

By

Donald K.Morgan

**Copyright © 2022 by
Donald K. Morgan**

All Rights Reserved.
No part of this book may be used or reproduced by any means, graphic, electronic, or mechanical, including photocopying, recording, taping, or by any information storage retrieval system without the written permission of the publisher.

Table of Content

INTRODUCTION

Chapter 1
Developing Your Business Idea

Chapter 2
Crafting a Business Plan

Chapter 3
Finding Funding For Your Business

Chapter 4
Registering Your Business

Chapter 5
Hiring Employees

Chapter 6
Setting up Your Business Location

Chapter 7
Creating a Brand and Logo

Chapter 8
Advertising and Marketing

Chapter 9
Growing and Scaling Your Business

INTRODUCTION

Welcome to Start Your Own Company: A Step-by-Step Guide to Run Your Own Company. This book is designed to provide you with the information, resources, and tools needed to start and successfully run your own business. Whether you're looking to start a new venture or are already operating a business, this guide will help you understand the process of launching and managing a business, from the initial planning stages to the day-to-day operations. With this book, you'll learn the basics of setting up a business, from choosing the right legal structure to registering with the appropriate authorities. You'll also get guidance on creating and managing a business plan, understanding and meeting financial obligations, and marketing your business. Additionally, you'll gain valuable insight into the best practices for managing personnel and operations. With this book, you'll have the knowledge and resources you need to get your business up and running.

Chapter 1

Developing Your Business Idea

Introduction

It is often said that the most successful businesses start with a great idea. Coming up with a business idea that is both innovative and feasible is often the first step in any successful venture. However, it can be difficult to know where to start when developing your business idea. This chapter will provide guidance on how to develop your business idea and provide some helpful tips on how to come up with an idea that is both unique and viable.

Brainstorming

The first step in developing your business idea is to brainstorm. This is the process of coming up with different ideas and concepts that could potentially be turned into a business. Brainstorming can be done alone or with a group of people, and it is important to think outside the box and consider all possibilities.
Brainstorming can be

done through a variety of methods, such as writing down ideas, drawing diagrams, or discussing potential ideas with others.

Research

Once you have a few ideas, it is important to do some research. This will help you determine if your idea is feasible and determine what needs to be done to make it a reality. Research should include looking into the industry, the competition, and the target market. Additionally, researching the legal and financial aspects of starting a business is also essential.

Validation

Once you have done your research, it is important to validate your business idea. Validation is the process of ensuring that your idea is viable and that there is a need for your product or service. This can be done through market research, such as surveys and interviews with potential customers or industry experts. Additionally, talking to potential investors or partners can also help you validate your business idea.

Business Model

Once you have validated your business idea, it is time to create a business model. A business model is a plan for how the business will operate, including the target market, pricing, and the marketing strategy. Additionally, a business model should also include a plan for scaling the business and a timeline for reaching certain milestones.

Conclusion

Developing a business idea is an essential part of starting a successful venture. This chapter has provided guidance

on how to develop your business idea, from brainstorming and researching to validating and creating a business model. It is important to remember that developing a business idea takes time and effort, but the rewards can be well worth it.

Chapter 2

Crafting a Business Plan

A business plan is an essential tool for any business, whether just starting up or already established. It helps to ensure that your business is on the right track and is achieving its goals.

Here are the steps to crafting a business plan:

1. *Research*: Research your industry, competitors and target market. This will help you better understand the environment you'll be operating in and also provide valuable insight for creating an effective business plan.

2. *Define Your Goals*: Outline your long-term

and short-term goals. This will help you stay focused and guide your decisions when writing the rest of the business plan.

3. *Outline Your Business Model*: Creating a clear business model will help you understand how your business will make money and what resources you need to succeed.

4. *Create a Financial Plan*: Compile your sales

forecasts and financial projections. This will help you understand what kind of cash flow you need to support your operations and growth.

5. *Write Your Business Plan:* Put all the information you've gathered into a comprehensive business plan. This should include an executive summary, company overview, market analysis, product/service overview, financials, and operations/management plan.

6. *Review & Revise*: Take the time to review your business plan and make revisions where needed. It's important to keep it updated as your business grows and changes.

By following these steps, you can craft a business

plan that will help you achieve success.

Chapter 3

Finding Funding For Your Business

Starting a business can be an exciting venture, but it can also be expensive. Funding your business can be a challenge, but with the right resources, you can find the capital you need to get your business up and running.

Here are some tips for finding funding for your business:

1. *Explore Traditional Sources of Funding*: The first place to look for funding is traditional sources such as banks, credit unions, and private lenders. Banks and credit unions usually offer loans and lines of credit to businesses that meet their requirements. Private lenders may also offer loans or investments in exchange for equity in the business.

2. *Consider Crowdfunding:* Crowdfunding is a popular option for businesses that need capital. Using websites such as Kickstarter, businesses can post campaigns and ask for donations from individuals. In exchange for donations, businesses can offer rewards such as products or services related to their business.

3. *Look for Grants and Incentives*:

Grants and incentives are available from government programs, foundations, and other organizations. These funds are often earmarked for specific industries or businesses, such as those that are creating jobs in a certain area or those that are developing innovative products.

4. *Utilize Your Network*: Your network of family, friends, and colleagues may be a great source of funding. They can provide advice and resources, as well as capital.

5. *Seek Out Angel Investors*: Angel investors are wealthy individuals who provide capital to small businesses in exchange for equity in the business. They may also provide mentoring and advice.

6. *Research Alternative Sources:*
Alternative sources of funding such as microloans and peer-to-peer lending are becoming increasingly popular. These sources of funding may offer lower interest rates and more flexible payment terms.

Finding funding for your business can be a challenge, but with the right resources, you can find the capital you need to get your business up and running. By exploring traditional sources of funding, considering crowdfunding, looking for grants and incentives, utilizing your network, seeking out angel investors, and researching alternative sources, you can find the funding you need to get your business off the ground.

Chapter 4

Registering Your Business

Before you can launch your business, you must register it with the appropriate state or local government agencies. The process of registering your business can vary depending on the type of business you are starting and the laws of your state or locale. Generally, however, the steps are similar and include the following:

1. *Choose a Business Name*:
The first step to registering your business is to choose a name. Depending on the type of business you are starting, you may need to register the name with the state or local government. The name you choose should

be unique and not already in use by another business. It should also be memorable and easy to spell.

2. *Register Your Business:* Once you have chosen a name, you must register your business with the appropriate government agency. Depending on the type of business you are starting, you may need to register with the Secretary of State, the Internal

Revenue Service (IRS), or your county or municipality. The registration process may include filing paperwork, paying registration fees, and obtaining any necessary permits or licenses.

3. *Obtain an Employer Identification Number (EIN):*
If you are starting a business that will have employees, you must

obtain an Employer Identification Number (EIN) from the IRS. An EIN is a unique nine-digit number used to identify your business for tax purposes. You can apply for an EIN online or by mail.

4. *Open a Business Bank Account*:
Once you have registered your business and obtained an EIN, you should open a business bank account. This will

help you keep your business and personal finances separate and make it easier to manage your finances.

5. *Set Up Accounting System:*
You should also set up an accounting system to help you track your business's income and expenses. There are many software programs available that can help you manage your accounts.

By following these steps, you can register your business and get it off the ground. Once your business is registered, you can begin to market and promote it and start making a profit.

Chapter 5

Hiring Employees

The process of hiring employees is one of the most important aspects of running a successful business. It is essential to find the right people to join your team and fill specific roles. In order to do so, employers must have an effective recruitment and selection process. This chapter will focus on how employers can effectively recruit, select, and onboard new employees.

Recruiting Employees: The first step in hiring employees is to develop a recruitment strategy. This involves defining the roles you need to fill, creating job descriptions, and advertising the positions. It is important to ensure that the job descriptions are accurate, clear, and attractive to potential applicants. Employers should also consider using recruitment software and online job boards to reach a wider applicant pool.

Screening and Selecting Employees:
Once applicants have been identified, they must be screened and selected to find the best candidate for the role. This is typically done through

interviewing, background checks, and reference checks. Employers should also consider using assessments, such as skills tests, to identify the best fit for the role.

Onboarding Employees: Once a candidate has been selected, employers must ensure they are properly onboarded. This involves providing orientation, training, and paperwork. It is essential to ensure that new employees understand their roles and have the necessary skills to be successful.

Conclusion:

Hiring employees is a critical process that can have a major impact on the success of a business. Employers must have an effective strategy for recruiting, selecting, and onboarding employees in order to find the best fit for their organization. By following the steps outlined above, employers can ensure they are making the right hiring decisions.

Chapter 6

Setting up Your Business Location

1. *Research Potential Locations*: Research the local market to identify potential locations for your business. Consider factors such as access to major roads, public transportation, available parking, nearby competitors, and the population of potential customers.

2. *Analyze Costs*: Take into account the monthly rent, real estate taxes, insurance, and any other costs associated with the space. Determine what is affordable for you and your business.

3. *Consider Zoning*: Make sure that the location you choose is in an area zoned for the type of business you plan to operate.

4. *Inspect the Property*: Check the condition of the property and the surrounding area. Make sure there are no safety hazards or environmental concerns.

5. *Negotiate Terms*: Once you have identified a potential location, negotiate terms with the landlord or property owner. This may include rent, length of lease, and other conditions.

6. *Finalize the Deal*: Sign a lease agreement and obtain any necessary permits and licenses. Make sure to read and understand any documents before signing.

7. *Prepare the Space*: Once you have secured the space, it's time to prepare it for your

business. This may include painting, renovating, and furnishing the space.

8. *Market the Location:* Make sure to market your new location to attract customers. This may include using social media, local advertising, and word-of-mouth.

By following these steps, you can set up your business location with ease. With a bit of research and planning, you can find the perfect spot for your business.

Chapter 7

Creating a Brand and Logo

Creating a brand and logo for your business is an essential part of establishing a successful business. A brand is how customers perceive your business and how it stands out from the competition. A logo is the visual representation of your brand and is used to create recognition and recall.

When creating your brand, consider what you want your business to stand for. Think about what makes it unique and how you want customers to feel when they think of your business. Use this to create a brand identity that is consistent across all of your materials.

When creating a logo, keep it simple and distinct. Stay away from complex designs and colors that may be difficult for customers to remember. Aim for a logo that is easy to understand and recognize, and one that reflects the values of your brand.

Your brand and logo should work together to create a unified and recognizable identity. This will help customers recognize and remember your business, and also help to set you apart from the competition.

Take your time when creating your brand and logo, as it is an important part of your business's success. Ensure that your brand and logo are consistent and recognizable, and that they accurately reflect your business's values and mission.

Creating a strong brand and logo will help you

establish a successful business.

Chapter 8

Advertising and Marketing

Advertising and marketing are essential to the success of any business. Without them, potential customers will never know your business exists. Here are some tips on how to effectively advertise and market your business.

1. *Identify Your Target Market:* Before you can begin to advertise and market your business, it is important to identify your target market. Who are you trying to reach? Determine the demographics of your target market, such as age, gender, location, etc., so that you can develop advertisements and marketing materials that will resonate with that audience.

2. Develop a Marketing Plan: Once you have identified your target market, you should create a comprehensive marketing plan. This plan should outline your goals and objectives, the strategies you plan to use to reach your target audience, and the timeline for implementation.

3. Utilize Digital Advertising: Digital

advertising is one of the best ways to reach potential customers. Utilize tools such as search engine optimization, pay-per-click advertising, and social media marketing to reach your target audience.

4. *Leverage Traditional Advertising*: Traditional forms of advertising, such as print, broadcast, and outdoor advertising, can still be effective for reaching potential customers. Consider using a combination of traditional and digital advertising to maximize your reach.

5. *Use Local Events:* Participating in local events, such as festivals and conferences, is a great way to connect with potential customers. These events provide an opportunity to meet people face-to-face and build relationships with them.

6. *Create Great Content*: Creating content that is relevant, interesting, and valuable to your target audience is essential for effective advertising and marketing. This content can include blog posts, videos, podcasts, and more.

7. *Measure and Analyze Results:* Tracking and

analyzing the results of your advertising and marketing efforts is important. Measure the success of each campaign, and make adjustments as needed to ensure you are getting the most out of your efforts.

Advertising and marketing are essential for any business to succeed. By following these tips, you can effectively reach your target audience and grow your business.

Chapter 9

Growing and Scaling Your Business

Growing and scaling a business involves taking steps to increase the size and efficiency of the operation. This could include expanding the customer base, increasing product lines, developing new marketing strategies, and increasing the number of employees. It also involves increasing the efficiency of operations, such as streamlining processes, adopting new technologies, and improving customer service. The goal is to increase the company's profits and market share while maintaining quality and customer satisfaction. In order to successfully scale a business, leadership must develop a strategic plan to determine the best way to expand. Additionally, the company must have sufficient capital to finance the growth, and must find ways to increase efficiency and reduce costs.

In many cases, scaling a business involves partnering with other companies or taking on investors. This allows the company to access additional resources, such as capital, expertise, and access to new markets. However, it is important to be sure that the partnerships are mutually beneficial and that the goals of both parties are aligned. Additionally, it is important to protect the company's assets and interests by ensuring that contracts are fair and in line with the company's long-term goals.

Finally, it is essential to have a clear vision for the future of the company and to have the right people in place to achieve success. This includes having the right team in place to lead the company's growth, having a clear strategy for scaling the business, and having the right tools and technologies in place to support the growth.

In conclusion,

 START YOUR OWN COMPANY: A Step By Step Guide to Run Your Own Company is an invaluable tool for aspiring entrepreneurs. It provides a comprehensive overview of the steps necessary to launch a successful business, from developing a business plan and securing funding to marketing and managing the daily operations. With this guide, entrepreneurs have the tools they need to hit the ground running and create a thriving and successful company.

www.ingramcontent.com/pod-product-compliance
Lightning Source LLC
Chambersburg PA
CBHW070312220526
45465CB00004B/1853